THIS IS THE MOST REMARKABLE MATERIAL FULL OF ALL ORIGINAL WAYS TO SCORE IN THE SINGLES MARKET, MAKE A STRONG STATEMENT AND INFLUENCE WOMEN OF ALL KINDS WITH THIS SOLID AND DIRECT WORKS OF WIT DESIGNED TO WIN HER OVER INSTANTLY.

PLAYERS INC.
101 WAYS TO SCORE

GIGGIN' JIG JAMESON

authorHOUSE®

AuthorHouse™
1663 Liberty Drive, Suite 200
Bloomington, IN 47403
www.authorhouse.com
Phone: 1-800-839-8640

First published by AuthorHouse 4/27/2010

ISBN: 978-1-4490-5675-9 (e)
ISBN: 978-1-4490-5674-2 (sc)

Printed in the United States of America
Bloomington, Indiana

This book is printed on acid-free paper.

A MANUAL
<u>CONTAINING REMARKABLE</u>
ALL ORIGINAL

* PICK UP LINES
AND
ENUENDOS

* ORIGINAL JOKES

* WORKS OF WIT

BONUS
MATERIAL

* HANDED DOWN JOKES
AND PICK UP LINES

* LYRICS

* POEM'S

* WORDS OF WISDOM

CONTENTS

PICK UP LINES AND ENUENDO'S

1*TAKE A RIDE ON MY BOLOGNA PONY, IT'S READY FOR YOUR SOFT BUNS

2* "LADY IN COFFEE SHOP" HOW ABOUT A LITTLE HALF N HALF SO WE CAN CREAM TOGETHER

3*HEY BABY MY LITTLE SOLDIER SALUTES YOU, HOW WOULD YOU LIKE TO POLISH MY HELMET

4*HOW WOULD YOU LIKE ME TO BE YOUR PERSONAL GINACOLOGIST NO STRINGS   ATTACHED, UNLESS YOU'RE ON THE PLUG THAT IS

5*I'M A CHARMIN MAN, YOU CAN SQUEEZE ME ANY TIME

6*I USED TO LAY PIPE, NOW I'M AN UNDERSIDE TECHNICIAN

7*HEY YOU HOT FAMALÉ, GIVE ME SOME SPICE

8* "FOR A WAITRESS"
I'LL TAKE A FIESTA WHORE PLATTER AND I'LL BE DAMNED SURE TO GIVE YOU A BIG TIP

9* "FOR A BABE SUNTANNING"
ARE YOU GOING FOR OVER-EASY OR SUNNY-SIDE UP
I JUST WANT TO GIVE YOU A HARD TIME BABE

10*I'M SIR-LOIN, NICE TO MEAT YOU

11*DAMN GIRL, YOU GOT A BOOT SCOOT CRAP SHOOT, ALL WE NEED IS A PAIR OF DICE (PARADISE) AND I CAN ROLL ON THAT ANY TIME

12*YOU LOOK AS GOOD COMING AS YOU DO GOING, YOU CAN LEAVE ME BEHIND ANYTIME

13*IS IT HOT IN HERE OR IS IT JUST YOU

*JUST CAUSE YOU'RE HOT DOESN'T MEAN YOU CAN BURN ME

14*I'M A MASTER BAITER AND I'M READY TO REEL YOU IN

15*I WOULD LIKE TO FLOAT MY BOAT DOWN YOUR LOVE CANAL

16*HEY HOW ABOUT YOU FLY DOWN SOUTH AND PLANT YOUR TULIPS

17*MY EX- LOVER TOLD ME I HAD TO GET IN TOUCH WITH MY INNER ASSHOLE, SO I TOOK IT LITERALLY

18* "BITCH BUMPS INTO YOU" YOU CAN BROAD SIDE ME ANY- TIME, BUT LOOK OUT 'CAUSE I MIGHT REAR END YOU TO EVEN THE SCORE

19*HOW WOULD YOU LIKE TO COME HOME AND MEET MY TWO BOYS AND THEIR DOG

20*I'M LOOKING AT YOU THROUGH MY WHORE SCOPE AND I'M WAITING FOR A SIGN

21* "A COUPLE GIRLFRIENDS TOGETHER"
HEY I BET YOU I CAN CUM BETWEEN YOU TWO. WHO SAYS THREES A CROWD, LET'S MAKE IT A LOVE TRIANGLE AND I MEAN TRY ANY ANGLE

22* "FLIPPING A QUARTER"
YOU GOT ME FLIPPIN' GIRL, WHAT'S
IT GONNA BE HEAD OR TAIL
I JUST WANT TO GIVE YOU A HARD
TIME BABE!

23*WHAT'S THE ROOT WORD OF
CAUCASIAN?

COCK-CAJUN STYLE

24**I'M GIGGIN' JIG JAMESON
I'M THE LOCAL KIELBASA AND I'M
LOCO IN THE CABEZA

25*IT'S TIME TO BUTTER THAT BUNGINA AND CREAM TOGETHER

26*IF YOU SHOOT ME DOWN WITH A "NO" JUST TURN THAT AROUND AND THE GAME IS "ON"

ORIGINAL JOKES

27*WHY DID THE HOOKER GO INTO THE BAIT SHOP?

CAUSE SHE HEARD SHE COULD REEL IN A MASTER BAITER

28*THE RAG WAS IN THE CLOSET SO I HAD TO TAKE HER OUT DESPITE HOW DIRTY SHE WAS

29*WHAT DID THE GIRL SAY AFTER THE GUY PROPOSED TO HER?

I CANTALOPE UNLESS YOU LOVE MY BIG MELONS

30*WHY DID THE EAGER BEAVER SAY, "DAMN IT"

CAUSE SHE HAD TO WORK SO HARD TO GET THE WOOD

31*WHAT'S THE GOOD THING ABOUT EATING PUSSY?

YOU CAN FLOSS YOUR TEETH WITH HER PUBES

32*GUESS WHY I WANT TO GO TO LAS VEGAS?

TO HIT THE MUST GET TANG RANCH AND PLAY THE SLUTS

33*WHAT DOES EVERY PRISONER POSSESS AFTER GETTING CON-VICTED BY THE BALLS?

A COUPLE ACHERS!!

34*WHYAREALLORIENTALPEOPLE NAMED AFTER MALE BODY PARTS, LIKE WANG, PANG, YANG, WONG AND DONG?!?!

35*WHERE DID THE GAY PHAROAH HIDE HIS TREASURE?

IN HIS SPHYNXTER

36*WHAT DO YOU PAY A MERMAID STRIPPER THAT WEARS A SEA CUP SIZE TOP/

YOU PAY HER WITH SAND DOLLARS

37*WHAT DO YOU CALL A COLD GLASS OF MILK?

UTTER DELIGHTMENT

38*A GUY MET A COW GIRL IN A BAR, SHE ASKED HIM "DO YOU LIKE COUNTRY?"

THE MAN SAID, "YEAH I LIKE A LITTLE CUNT TREE IN MY BACKYARD"

39*HOW MANY DUMB BLONDES DOES IT TAKE TO SCREW IN A LIGHT BULB?

ONE, BUT SHE WOULD RATHER DO IT IN PRIVATE

40*THIS GUY MET A SLUTTY BITCH IN A BAR. AFTER A ONE NIGHT STAND HE COMPLAINED TO HIS FRIENDS THAT SHE STUNK. "WHY?" THEY ASKED.

CAUSE SHE DOESN'T DO SHIT!! GET IT, DOUCHE IT

41*WHO WANTS TO BE MY LAZY, LAUGHING, LOVER?

MARY WANNA

42*AN EAGER MARRRIED WOMAN WAS INTERVIEWING A YOUNG MAN TO PUT UP A GAZEEBO IN HER BACK YARD. SHE ASKED HIM IF HE COULD ERECT SOME   WOOD.

HE SAID "I'M CONFIDENT I COULD NAIL HER DOWN AND KNOCK HER UP IN NO TIME"

43*WHAT DO YOU CALL IT WHEN A DRUNK SLUT GIVES YOU A BLOW JOB?

A PARTY FAVOR

44*A GAY GUY WALKS INTO A BAR AND ASK'S THE BARTENDER ,"HEY FILL ME UP WITH A NICE STIFF ONE." THE BARTENDER ALSO A FAG SAYS, "WOULD YOU ALSO LIKE ME TO PUSH IN YOUR STOOL?"

45*A DEPRESSED MAN SAT DOWN AT A BAR COMPLAINING HOW HIS WIFE RAN AWAY WITH THE MAIL MAN. THE BARTENDER SAID SARCASTICALLY, "WOULD YOU FEEL BETTER IF IT WAS THE MILK MAN INSTEAD?" THE DISTROUGHT MAN SNAPPED BACK, "YOU WOULD BE TESTEE TOO IF YOUR LIL' SMOKEY DIDN'T HAVE A BUN

46*A MAN AND A WIFE WERE ARGUING AND SHE YELLED OUT,"YOU'RE A PIECE OF SHIT!!" THE MAN SAID, "THAT'S <u>DEFIC</u>ATION OF CHARACTER," AT THE SAME TIME KICKING A GARBAGE CAN. SHE SAID, "SEE YOU KICKED THAT CAN FOR NO REASON!" HE EXCLAIMED, "LIKE YOU IT WAS TALKING TRASH AND FLIPPING IT'S LID!!"

47*HAVE YOU SEEN THE NEW MOVIE, "STAR WHORES," FEATUR-ING DARTH PANTY INVADER, WHO PIMPS PRINCESS LAYA LOT, TOO TRICK HAND SOLO AND LUKE STREET WALKER?

48*A MAN IN A CONFESSIONAL TOLD THE PRIEST, "MY MARRIAGE IS FAILING, I LOST MY JOB, AND MY DOG DIED" THE PRIEST ANSWERED, "YOU MUST HAVE FAITH AND HOPE AND LOTS OF PATIENCE" THE MAN REPLIED, "THAT'S WHAT STARTED THIS MESS. I HAD FAITH BENT OVER THE KITCHEN SINK, HOPE SPREAD ON THE BED AND IRONICALLY I HAVE MORE PATIENTS THAN THE MAYO CLINIC"

49*A MAN MET WITH HIS BOSS ABOUT TRYING TO GET A RAISE BECAUSE HE FEELS UNAPRECIATED. THE MAN EXCLAIMED, "IT'S TIME TO DEAL WITH THE MATTER AT HAND, YOUR JERKING ME OFF FOR PEANUTS AND YOU CRACKED THE WRONG NUT. DO YOU WANT TO SEE NUTS?! I'LL SHOW YOU NUTS!" THE BOSS SAID, "YOU'RE RIGHT, YOU SOLD ME WITH YOUR ANALOGIES AND SINCE THE ROOT WORD OF ANALOGIES IS ANAL, YOU WILL FIT IN JUST FINE, SO NOW I GUESS YOU'LL HAVE A GOOD PLACE TO STICK YOUR PEN"

50*WHY DID THE MEAN OLD MAN HARRASS THE NICE LADY?
BECAUSE **HER ASS** WOULDN'T QUIT!

51*WHAT ARE THE REQUIREMENTS FOR A HOOKER TO WORK IN A CAT HOUSE?

SHE'S GOTTA HAVE THE WHORE MOANS

52*WHAT DO YOU CALL A CROSS BETWEEN A CHICKEN AND A BUFFALO?

A CHIC-A-LO

53*WHAT DO YOU CALL AN AGREEMENT BETWEEN BOTH HEADS TO PURSUE ONLY BODACIOUS BLONDE BITCHES?

TO RECTIFY A BONERFIED PENAL CODE

54*A MAN SITS ON THE COUCH AND WATCHES A FOOTBALL GAME WITH HIS NUTS HANGING OUT OF HIS SHORTS. HIS WIFE SAYS, "STOP HANGING OUT AND BE AN ATHLETIC SUPPORTER!

55*WHAT DO YOU CALL IT WHEN A FAT, DUMB, HORNY COUNTRY GIRL GOES TO A PARTY?

A HO-DOWN

56*A COUPLE WERE ON A DATE AND THE MAN SAID, "YOU'RE KIND OF QUIET, CAN YOU REALLY FEEL MY PRESENCE LIKE THAT?" THE WOMAN SAID, "NO, FEEL YOUR OWN PRESENTS"

57*HOW DO YOU CONVINCE A PROSTITUTE TO GO CELIBATE?

TELL HER THAT HER JOHN WAS DOWN WITH NEIL AND BOB

58*WHAT'S THE WORST ADVICE TO GIVE A SUICIDAL PERSON?

HANG IN THERE PAL!!

59*I BET YOU DID'NT KNOW THAT INDIANS STARTED SCALPING POTATOES BEFORE PEOPLE

60*IF YOU'RE SICK OF PLAYING SPADES, PLAY A HO!

61*I WOULD KICK YOUR ASS BUT I WOULD PROBABLY MISTAKE IT FOR YOUR HEAD

62*WHAT DO YOU GIVE YOUR GIRLFRIEND FOR VALENTINES DAY?

THE GIFT THAT KEEPS ON GIVING, A RAGING CASE OF HERPES

63*A TRANSIENT WALKS INTO A BAR FOR THE FIRST TIME, THE BARTENDER SAID, "WHAT WILL IT BE?" THE BUM ANSWERED, "HOW ABOUT SOME RUM FOR A GLUM BUM. TAKE ME TO YOUR LITER"

64*IF ENGLAND IS RULED BY A MONARCHY, WHAT DO THEY DO WHEN ALL THE BUTTERFLIES MIGRATE?

THEY LET THE BUTTER FLY AT THE QUEEN

65 THEY CALL ME AN UNDERACHIEVER BUT AT LEAST I HAVE A PAIR OF NUTS UNDER MY BELT

66*WHY DID THE GUY GET ON A HORSE HALFWAY THROUGH THE FOOTRACE?

CAUSE HE COULDN'T HANDLE THE AGONY OF DEFEAT

67*WHAT DO YOU CALL A CRIMINAL WITH LEPROSY?

A LEPRECHAUN

68*EVERY ONE SHOULD HAVE A MONKEY ON THEIR BACK, WHO ELSE WOULD YOU GET TO EAT THE CHIP ON YOUR SHOULDER

69*A GUY CAME UP TO BAT IN A BALL GAME WHEN THE OTHER TEAMMATES SHOUTED, "DON'T WHIFF IT, JUST POKE IT IN THE GAP!!" THE BATTER WATCHED THREE STRIKES GO BY AND THE CATCHER FROM THE OTHER TEAM SAID, "THAT BATTER MUST REALLY STINK BECAUSE MY PITCHER JUST FANNED HIS ASS"

70*TWO DEAD HEADS WERE SMOKING A JOINT AND ONE OF THEM SAID, "THIS IS REALLY BORING, LIKE ACTUALLY BORING MY BRAIN INSANE" THE OTHER ONE LAUGHED AND SAID, "YOU'RE BURNT OUT MAN" THE OTHER GUY ANSWERED, "YEAH BUT PLUG ME INTO THE NEAREST OUTLET AND I'M AS GOOD AS NEW

71*DO YOU KNOW WHY THEY CALL HER A FEMALE?

CAUSE SHE'S OUR COMPANION FOR A FEE

72*WHAT DO YOU CALL AN UNDERACHIEVING, STUBBORN, DRUG ADDICTED, TREE HUGGER?

SLUFF THE TRAGIC PAGAN

73*WHATS THE GOOD THING ABOUT BEING THE LAST IN LINE?

CUZ YOUR ALWAYS CUMING UP THE REAR

74*WHAT DO YOU CALL A SQUAT IN NEW ORLEANS?

SOUTHERN CUMFORT

75*WHY DO PEOPLE GO FISHING IN SAN DIEGO?

JUST FOR THE HALIBUT

76* IF ALL YOU GOT IS A POT TO PISS IN, ANTEE UP CUZ URINE WITH A FLUSH

<u>WORKS OF WIT</u>

77*I CAN'T BELIEVE THAT OUT OF A MILLION SPERM YOU WERE THE QUICKEST ONE

78*<u>DEFIC</u>ATION OF CHARACTER IS MORE THAN JUST TALKING SHIT

79*YOU KNOW WHEN YOU'RE LOST WHEN NOW HERE BECOMES NOWHERE AND THE SPACE IN BETWEEN IS IN YOUR HEAD

80*YOU MUST LOSE YOUR MIND IN ORDER TO FREE YOUR SOUL

81*IT'S TIME TO DEAL WITH THE MATTER AT HAND!! QUIT JERKING ME OFF

82*YOU PUT THE "WO" IN WOMAN AND IT'S IRONIC THAT WO OR WOE MEANS TO BRING GREAT GRIEF AND DISAPPOINTMENT TO, THUS BE WOMAN

83*IF YOU'RE IN THE MIDDLE OF BELIEVING, YOU'RE LIVING A LIE

84*IF YOU LET YOURSELF "SOB" YOU ARE A REAL SON OF A BITCH

85*THE ONLY KIND OF PEACE THAT SELLS IS A PIECE OF ASS

86*WHAT'S THE DIFFERENCE BETWEEN OBAMA AND OSAMA? THE B & S

87*THOSE WITH KNOWLEDGE MUST KNOW THE LEDGE

88*IT DOESN'T TAKE A MICROBIOLOGIST TO SPLIT HAIRS

89*IF YOU EARN IN LIFE YOU WILL URN IN DEATH

90*BITCHES ARE ABOUT GABBIN' AND GUYS ARE ABOUT JABBIN'

91*PARADOX; I FEAR NOTHING AND IT'S NOTHING THAT I FEAR

92*HE WHO PINCHES PENNIES HAS GOOD CENTS

93*YOU CAN'T GET BLOOD FROM A TURNIP UNLESS YOU FELL OFF THE TURNIP TRUCK YESTERDAY

94*FLEECED LIKE A LAMB OF GOD, TO BE CHASED DOWN AND HERD BY A BACKWARDS DOG

95*MY GIRLFRIEND FROM BOISE SAYS, "<u>IDAHO</u> WITH THE BIGGEST SPUDS," AND SHE LIKES GETTING BAKED

96*A BIG MOUTH IS A SIGN OF FEAR AND IGNORANCE

97*THE WORD ENUENDO IS POETIC IRONY DESCRIBING IT'S OWN SEXUAL MEANING LIKE A SNAKE DEVOURING ITSELF

98*PARADOX; KEEP YOUR NOSE CLEAN, IN ORDER TO DO THAT AND GET CREDIT FOR IT, YOU MUST STICK YOUR NOSE UP SOMEONES ASS AND BROWN NOSE

99*THOSE WHO AREN'T PLAYING WITH A FULL DECK MUST BLUFF

100*SHAKESPEARE SAID, "TO BE OR NOT TO BE THAT IS THE QUESTION?" I SAY, "<u>WHEN</u> TO BE

AND <u>WHEN</u> NOT TO BE, THAT'S THE
ANSWER TO THE QUESTION!!"

101*CONTROLLED CHAOS, IS IT
JUST A PARADOX OR AN ESSENTIAL
DISPLACEMENT OF ENERGY
THAT EXPANDS AND CONTRACTS
RESULTING IN POWERFUL TIES
WITHIN THE FABRIC OF TIME AND
SPACE, THIS ULTIMATELY CREATES
ORDER IN THE UNIVERSE

*** BONUS MATERIAL ***

IF I TOLD YOU,YOU HAVE A NICE BODY WOULD YOU HOLD IT AGAINST ME.

YOU MUST BE TIRED CUZ YOU'VE BEEN RUNNING THROUGH MY HEAD ALL NIGHT.

WHAT DOES AN OLD LADIES PUSSY SMELL LIKE?

DEPENDS.

WHATS BETTER THAN ROSES ON A PIANO?

TULIPS ON AN ORGAN.

WHAT DO YOU CALL A TRUCK LOAD FULL OF VIBRATORS?

TOYS FOR TWATS.

HOW DID DAIRY QUEEN GET PREGNANT?

BURGER KING FORGOT TO WRAP ITS WHOPPER.

IF A YOUNG WHORE USES VASELINE, WHAT DOES AN OLD WHORE USE?

POLYGRIP.

WHAT DO YOU CALL A VIRGIN IN GERMAN?

GOOD-N-TIGHT

WHAT DID THE SIGN SAY IN THE BAR WINDOW?

LIQUOR IN THE FRONT/ POKER IN THE REAR.

A BACKWORDS MOOD LEADS TO CERTAIN DOOM.

THOSE WHO BELIEVE IN SODOMITES. ARE A REAL PAIN IN THE ASS!

DON'T BLOW SMOKE UP MY ASS CUZ I'LL JUST BLOW SMOKE RINGS

EVIL IS RIGHT AND CHAOS IS LEFT

WHAT'S SIMPLE YET COMPLEX?

SEX WITH A SIMPLEX

HAIL THE DARK ONE

VERSE:
JUST GOT LAID ON A FRIDAY NIGHT
FOUND A 20 DOLLAR BILL OUT-A-
SIGHT. LIVING LARGE BRING ON
THAT FIGHT.

CHORUS:
PLEASURES OF THE FLESH O' SO
FUN. PULL THAT SHADE ON THE
SUN. HAIL THE DARK ONE... HAIL
THE DARK ONE... HAIL THE DARK
ONE.

VERSE:
FIND A VIRGIN STRIP HER CLOTHES,
KILL TO OFFER BOUNDLESS SOULS.
MAKE HER THE ALTAR GIRL, GIVE
IT A WHIRL, LET THE DARK ONE
RULE THIS WORLD.

WAY TO HIGH TO PAY, TOO DAMN DRUNK TO STAY. RESPECTS TO PAY FOR THE LATE GREAT ANTON LAVEY.

WALK TO THE LEFT OR TO THE RIGHT. PREY ON THE WEAK OF ETERNAL NIGHT CHEATING DEATH WITH A WOODEN STAKE. TELL ME NOW WHICH PATH WILL YOU TAKE.

CHORUS:
PLEASURES OF THE FLESH O' SO FUN. PULL THAT SHADE ON THE SUN. HAIL THE DARK ONE... HAIL THE DARK ONE... HAIL THE DARK ONE.

VERSE:
DID A LITTLE LADY, DONE BY NOON GET 'EM ALL TOGHETHER AND SHOOT THE SPOON. LOAD THE RIG WATCH YOUR BACK DON'T

MATTER IF IT'S CRANK OR SMACK DON'T YOU WORRY IF NEEDLES ARE NOT YOUR KICK, THERE ARE PLENTY OF POISONS TO TAKE YOUR PICK. UP ALL NIGHT YOU'RE FELLING KINDA SPUN. IT'S DOG EAT DOG DON'T FORGET YOUR GUN. IT'S TIME TO

GRIND YOUR GROOVE 'TIL THE MIDNIGHT MOVES. WALK A MILE IN YOUR CLOVEN HOOVES. LEARN TO LIVE THE POWER OF A PUN. SELL YOUR SOUL AND HAIL THE DARK ONE.

CHORUS:
PLEASURES OF THE FLESH O' SO FUN. PULL THAT SHADE ON THE SUN. HAIL THE DARK ONE... HAIL THE DARK ONE... HAIL THE DARK ONE.

VERSE:
FIND A VIRGIN STRIP HER CLOTHES, KILL TO OFFER BOUNDLESS SOULS. MAKE HER THE ALTAR GIRL, GIVE IT A WHIRL, LET THE DARK ONE RULE THIS WORLD.

WAY TO HIGH TO PAY, TOO DAMN DRUNK TO STAY. RESPECTS TO PAY FOR THE LATE GREAT ANTON LAVEY.

CHORUS:
PLEASURES OF THE FLESH O' SO FUN. PULL THAT SHADE ON THE SUN. HAIL THE DARK ONE... HAIL THE DARK ONE... HAIL THE DARK ONE.

HIGH ON THE HOG

CHORUS:
I'M SITTING HIGH ON THE HOG I WILL PREVAIL. SPROUT ME SOME WINGS AND GROW ME A TAIL. IT'S TIME TO FEED THE FIRE, THROW ON ANOTHER LOG. I'M BIDING MY TIME , I'M SITTING HIGH ON THE HOG. ROLLING THUNDER I'M HIGH ON THE HOG. POUNDING PAVEMENT I'M HIGH ON THE HOG, HIGH... HIGH...HIGH...HIGH ON THE HOG.

VERSE:
SOFTTAIL, FATBOY, SUPERGLIDE, SPORT, WILD WILD WOMEN IN EVERY PORT. CREAM PIES AND CHROME PIPES HEY HEY HONEY YOU'RE JUST MY TYPE. HOP ON BACK WE'LL TEAR UP THE STREET, GIRLS GONE WILD, THAT'S MY KIND OF FREAK, WE'LL MAKE IT ,

WE'LL SHAKE IT, BITCH WE WON'T EVEN FAKE IT.

YOUR GROOVES AND CURVES EXCITE MY NERVES. I AM THE LORD OF LUST AND I'M HERE TO BITE SOME BUSTS.

CHORUS:
I'M SITTING HIGH ON THE HOG I WILL PREVAIL. SPROUT ME SOME WINGS AND GROW ME A TAIL. IT'S TIME TO FEED THE FIRE, THROW ON ANOTHER LOG. I'M BIDING MY TIME , I'M SITTING HIGH ON THE HOG. ROLLING THUNDER I'M HIGH ON THE HOG. POUNDING PAVEMENT I'M HIGH ON THE HOG, HIGH... HIGH...HIGH...HIGH ON THE HOG.

VERSE:
TO BE FLEECED LIKE A LAMB OF GOD, TO BE CHASED DOWN AND HERD BY A BACKWORDS DOG. SPILL THE GUTS AND SLAUGHTER THEIR

NUTS, KILL THE SCAPEGOAT AND ROCK THE BOAT. FLEECED VIRGIN WOOL TAKEN FROM THE LAMB OF GOD. THE ULTIMATE SACRAFICE DECAPITATION ON A LOG. ONE LAST SURGE IN WHICH WE EMERGE, BORN FROM THICK FOG WE'RE SITTING HIGH ON THE HOG.

CHORUS:
I'M SITTING HIGH ON THE HOG I WILL PREVAIL. SPROUT ME SOME WINGS AND GROW ME A TAIL. IT'S TIME TO FEED THE FIRE, THROW ON ANOTHER LOG. I'M BIDING MY TIME , I'M SITTING HIGH ON THE HOG. ROLLING THUNDER I'M

HIGH ON THE HOG. POUNDING PAVEMENT I'M HIGH ON THE HOG, HIGH... HIGH...HIGH...HIGH ON THE HOG.

VERSE:
BODACIOUS BITCH WITH THE BOOT SCOOT CRAP SHOOT. SHE'S GOT THE PAIR-A-DICE AND THAT ROLL OF LOOT. PICK A TABLE AND PUT ON MY LUCKY HAT, LIGHT UP A SMOKE AND BABY I CAN ROLL ON THAT. SHAKE A MARTINI WITH AN OLIVE AND ICE, THE NIGHT IS LONG WITH THAT PARADISE. ROCK 'N' ROLL WITH THAT LUCKY SEVEN BOOT SCOOT SHAKIN IN A CRAP SHOOT HEAVEN.

CHORUS:
BITCH WE'RE SITTING HIGH ON THE HOG, WE WILL PREVAIL. SPROUT ME SOME WINGS AND GROW ME A TAIL. IT'S TIME TO FEED THE FIRE, THROW ON ANOTHER LOG. I'M BIDING MY TIME, I'M SITTING HIGH ON THE HOG. ROLLING THUNDER

WE'RE HIGH ON THE HOG.

POUNDING PAVEMENT I'M HIGH ON THE HOG, TEARING IT UP WE'RE SITTING HIGH ON THE HOG, HIGH ON THE HOG, UNTIL THE SWEET SWEET END WE'RE HIGH ON THE HOG. HIGH...HIGH...HIGH...HIGH ON THE FUCKING HOG.

BITCH IN HEAT

VERSE:
WAGGING YOUR TAIL DOWN BY MY FEET, SLOPPY WET KISSES LIKE A BITCH IN HEAT. DO YOU DOGGY-STYLE AND SECRETE THE FLEET, HORNY LITTLE BITCH STICKING OUT YOUR SEAT. GETTING REAL HOT LIKE A BITCH IN HEAT. I'LL BEND YOU OVER A LOG AND FUCK YOU LIKE A DOG. ALL I SEE IS YOUR BIG ROUND BACKSIDE, DON'T SHOW ME YOUR FACE OR I'LL RUN AND HIDE. IT'S TIME TO FREAK YOUR CHEEKS CUZ IT'S NOT THE FACE I'M FUCKING IT'S THE FUCK I'M FACING. HOT AND HEAVY ON NEIGHBORHOOD TRICKS, SETTING OUT THAT ASS FOR NEIGHBORHOOD PRICKS. RYTHMIC PASSION PUMPING PURE PLEASURE MUTUAL MOANING AND MOVING TOGETHER. I ALWAYS MIX BUSINESS WITH PLEASURE, WE'LL CUM TOGETHER AND SHARE THE TREASURE.

BUST A NUT

VERSE:
THROW HER ON THE BED AND CALL HER A SLUT, DO HER DOGGYSTYLE AND CUM IN HER BUTT. GO ON AND BUST A NUT IN THE CRACK OF HER BUTT. DIG HER DOGGYSTYLE AND SMACK HER LIKE A MUTT. BUMP AND GRIND UNTIL YOU BUST A NUT. RULE THAT RUMP LIKE A ROYAL RED TRUMP. DO THE BUMP AND HUMP AND SHOW HER YOU AIN'T NO CHUMP. BIG TITS AND TINY CLITS, STICKING MY DICK WHERE EVER IT FITS. NIBBLE AND LICK THAT JUICY CLIT, COMING UP NOW TO TAKE A HIT. GET PASSED THE SMELL AND YOU GOT IT LICKED. LICKITY SPLIT LET ME KISS THAT CLIT. SEXY MAMA WITH THE BIG ROUND TITS. SCREAMING FULL BOAR ORGASM, SCREAMING WHORES ON THE FLOOR IN SPAZM.

SOUTHERN BELLE

VERSE:
IT JUST MAY BE ALL THAT YOU KNOW. I'LL TELL YOU RIGHT NOW YOU GIVE A HELL OF A BLOW. CROSS EYED BITCH LIKE A DEEP THROAT PRO, TURNING TRICKS LIKE A SALTY HO. IT'S THE ONLY THING YOU COULD POSSIBLY SELL ONE WAY TICKET TO A LIVING HELL. TURNING TRICKS FOR MONEY, DON'T YOU KNOW YOU'RE EVERYBODIES HONEY. YOU CLAIM TO SEE THE LIGHT BUT IT AIN'T EVEN SUNNY. LITTLE BITCH GET ON YOUR KNEES DO THE KNEEL AND BOB YOU FUCKING TEASE.

GOOD FRIENDS

GOOD FRIENDS ARE NOT COMMODITIES ON SUPER MARKET SHELVES. ALL NEATLY PRICED AND PACKAGED SO FOLKS CAN HELP THEMSELVES. THEY DON'T COME BY THE DOZEN, THEIR NOT SOLD BY THE POUND. TO GET THE BEST IN QUALITY IT PAYS TO SHOP AROUND. OH YES WE WANT OUR FRIENDS TO COME COMPLETELY GUARANTEED,TO LAST US FOR A LIFETIME AND FULL FILL OUR EVERY NEED. WHILE WERE BUSY SHOPPING FOR THE FRIENDS WHO'LL SUIT US BEST DO WE EVER STOP TO WOUDER IF WE TOO CAN PASS THE TEST. HOW MUCH WILL WE CONTRIBUTE, WHAT EFFORT WILL WE MAKE TO ACT AND HELP AND COMFORT AND GIVE AS WELL AS TAKE.

APOCALYPTIC SOW

A CRYSTALINE CROSS OF BUNGLE IN THE JUNGLE, A GIANT BEE CALLED BUMBLE. A SLIGHT SWERVE CAUSES A TUMBLE FOR FAN FAIR OF DREADED DEAD HEADS AND BEATNIKS. BORING THROUGH MIST OF A PLACE THEY CALL THE STYX. TRAVELING ALL TOGETHER IN THE NICEST OF WEATHER. FEEDING THE BEAST THINGS MADE OF LEATHER. SHOOTING AT BUGS SCORING POINTS, ALL THE DAY WHILE FIENDING ON JOINTS. NEARING THEIR TEMPLE THEY LONG FOR LIFE SIMPLE LIKE RELEASING THEIR SOULS WITH THE POP OF A PIMPLE. IN TIME WAY AMPLE THEY REFUSE TO BE AN EXAMPLE. CHANTING TO THEIR LORD THE HEADS DRAW THEIR SWORDS, WHO WOULD KNOW IT'S A
MAN'S DREAM IN A WARD. THINGS

HE CAN THINK OF WHEN HE IS BORED. THE FANTASY CONTINUES CAUSE HE IS BEING USED. A SPIDER THEY FIGHT YOU KNOW THEY CAN'T LOSE, INTO THE NIGHT THE SPIDER'S GUTS OOZE, WOUNDS YOU CAN'T MEND EVEN WITH BOOZE. THE SPIDER DEAD AND THE FREAKS JUST BRUISED. IT'S ALWAYS A BATTLE WHEN YOU'RE IN THE SYSTEM. LITTLE DID HE KNOW THE NURSE JUST FRISKED HIM. THE DREAM IS OVER NOW. IF IT WASN'T FOR THAT APOCALYPTIC SOW.

RELUCTANT SPARROW

THERE ONCE WAS A RELUCTANT SPARROW WHO DIDN'T FLY SOUTH FOR THE WINTER . HE SOON GOT CAUGHT IN THE SLEET AND SNOW AND HIS WINGS FROZE. FALLING TO THE EARTH HE LANDED IN A BARN.NEARLY FROZEN TO DEATH A COW SHIT ON HIM. SOON HE WAS HAPPILY SINGING IN THE PILE OF SHIT,WHEN A TOM CAT APPEARED, UNCOVERED HIM FROM THE SHIT AND PROMPTLY ATE HIM. THERE ARE THREE LESSONS TO BE LEARNED FROM THIS. NOT EVERYBODY THAT SHITS ON YOU IS YOUR ENEMY. NOT EVERYBODY THAT GET'S YOU OUT OF SHIT IS YOUR FRIEND. AND WHEN YOUR WARM AND HAPPY IN A PILE OF SHIT KEEP YOUR MOUTH SHUT.

About the Author

I am a man of both vision and experience that has been playing the field as if it were a Job for years. I have mastered the first impression with this collection of all original pick up lines, jokes, and works of wit. I am a player of another league that has passed his abilities on to you.